Deepfake Detection & AI Identity Fraud

Stopping AI-Powered Impersonation, Scams & Digital Forgery

By Joe Correa

Published by Live Stronger Faster

This book is for educational and informational purposes only. The author and publisher are not engaged in rendering legal, financial, tax, or other professional advice. Readers should consult a qualified professional before making any financial decisions.

First Edition

Table of Contents

Introduction

The digital world is entering an era where seeing is no longer believing. For centuries, human society has relied on visual and audio evidence as the foundation of trust. A photograph, a recorded voice, a live video call, or a signed document were once considered reliable proof of identity and truth. Today, artificial intelligence has shattered that assumption. Anyone with access to modern AI tools can fabricate a person's face, voice, handwriting, and mannerisms with astonishing realism. Deepfakes are no longer a novelty reserved for viral memes and movie studios. They have become one of the most powerful cyber-weapons ever created, capable of destroying reputations, stealing fortunes, manipulating elections, and collapsing businesses in minutes. This book exists because digital identity itself is now under attack, and the consequences reach far beyond technology.

Deepfake technology is advancing at an exponential pace. What once required a team of engineers and weeks of processing can now be accomplished in seconds using consumer-grade software or cloud-based AI platforms. Criminal organizations, state-sponsored hackers, fraud rings, and even lone actors are using these tools to impersonate CEOs, politicians, celebrities, and ordinary people alike. A voice cloned from a few seconds of audio can authorize bank transfers, bypass security protocols, and convince employees to release confidential data. A fake video can destroy someone's credibility or spark social unrest before the truth ever has a chance to catch up. AI identity fraud is not a future risk. It is a present-day crisis reshaping crime, cybersecurity, and human trust itself.

Unlike traditional cybercrime, deepfake attacks do not target servers or software first. They target people. They exploit the most powerful vulnerability in every system: human belief. When an employee sees their boss on a video call instructing them to wire money, or hears a loved one begging for help on the phone, logic is replaced by emotion. AI-generated content is engineered to trigger urgency, fear, and authority. These attacks bypass firewalls, encryption, and antivirus software because the victim willingly gives the attacker what they want. This is why deepfakes represent a new category of cyber threat—one that merges psychological manipulation with digital forgery at scale.

The financial damage from AI identity fraud is already reaching into the billions. Businesses have lost millions in single incidents where deepfake voices were used to authorize fraudulent payments. Individuals have had their life savings drained after scammers cloned a family member's voice.

Companies have been blackmailed with fabricated videos of executives engaging in criminal or embarrassing behavior. Governments are facing foreign influence campaigns driven by synthetic media designed to destabilize democracies. As AI becomes more sophisticated, these attacks will grow faster, cheaper, and harder to detect. Every organization, from a small business to a multinational corporation, is now exposed.

Deepfakes also pose a profound legal and ethical crisis. Courts, banks, insurance companies, and law enforcement agencies depend on digital evidence to establish identity and intent. But when video, audio, and images can be fabricated perfectly, how do you prove what is real? How do you authenticate a witness, a confession, or a transaction? How do you protect a person's likeness, voice, and biometric identity when AI can reproduce them flawlessly? The legal system is struggling to keep pace with a technology that is rewriting the rules of evidence, consent, and ownership. This book will show how deepfake detection is becoming one of the most important pillars of modern cybersecurity and digital law.

In this volume, you will learn how deepfake technology works, how it is created, and how it is weaponized. You will explore the AI models behind facial reenactment, voice synthesis, and synthetic avatars. You will see how criminals harvest images, videos, and audio from social media to build digital clones of their victims. You will understand how phishing has evolved into something far more dangerous: identity replication. The goal is not simply to trick someone, but to become them digitally. Once attackers control a convincing digital version of you, they can open accounts, reset passwords, request wire transfers, and manipulate others in your name.

You will also learn how defenders fight back. AI can be used not only to create deepfakes, but to detect them. Modern cybersecurity teams deploy machine-learning models that analyze micro-expressions, lighting inconsistencies, audio waveforms, eye movement patterns, and biological signals to identify synthetic media. Governments and financial institutions are investing heavily in biometric verification, liveness detection, cryptographic watermarking, and content authentication systems. This book will explain how these technologies work and how they are being deployed to protect digital identity at scale. The future of trust will not be based on what looks real, but on what can be mathematically verified.

Deepfake detection is not just for cybersecurity professionals. It is becoming a necessary skill for executives, lawyers, journalists, educators, parents, and everyday users. Anyone who communicates, transacts, or builds a personal brand online is now at risk. If your face, voice, or name has value, it can be exploited. That includes entrepreneurs, influencers, financial professionals, real estate agents, healthcare providers, and public figures of every kind. Even private individuals are vulnerable, as attackers increasingly use AI identity fraud for extortion, romance scams, and financial theft. The ability to verify who you are speaking to will soon be as important as locking your front door.

This book also explores the geopolitical dimension of deepfakes. Nation-states are using AI-generated media as part of information warfare campaigns. Fake speeches, staged videos, and fabricated news reports are being deployed to manipulate public opinion, undermine trust in institutions, and influence elections. The line between cyberwarfare and psychological warfare is disappearing. Deepfakes are becoming weapons of mass deception. Understanding how they work and how they are detected is no longer optional for anyone concerned with national security or democratic stability.

By the end of this book, you will understand the full landscape of AI-powered identity fraud. You will know how deepfakes are created, how they spread, how they deceive, and how they are detected. You will see how organizations build layered defenses that combine AI analysis, human verification, cryptographic signatures, and zero-trust identity systems. You will learn how to protect yourself, your business, and your digital reputation in a world where your likeness can be copied and weaponized. This knowledge is no longer technical trivia—it is survival training for the digital age.

Deepfakes represent one of the greatest threats to truth ever invented. But they also represent one of the greatest opportunities for cybersecurity innovation. As attackers evolve, defenders must evolve faster. This book stands at the front line of that battle. In the pages ahead, you will gain the tools, insight, and strategic understanding needed to fight back against the most dangerous form of cybercrime yet created: the theft of identity itself.

Chapter 1

The Rise of Synthetic Identity

The digital identity of every human being has become one of the most valuable assets in the modern economy. Your face, your voice, your signature, your writing style, your behavior patterns, and even the way you pause when you speak are now data points that can be collected, analyzed, and reproduced by artificial intelligence. This transformation did not happen suddenly. It grew quietly as social media, video platforms, smartphones, and cloud storage systems accumulated trillions of images, voices, and personal recordings. What was once casual content shared for entertainment or connection has become the raw material for synthetic identity systems that can reconstruct a human being digitally with terrifying accuracy.

Synthetic identity is the fusion of multiple data sources into a living digital replica. Unlike traditional identity theft, which steals a credit card number or social security number, AI identity fraud steals the person themselves. It captures how someone looks, sounds, moves, and thinks, then recreates it in software. With just a few minutes of video or audio, modern AI models can generate a voice that passes biometric verification, produce a face that reacts in real time, and mimic emotional expressions convincingly enough to deceive even close friends and family. This is no longer experimental technology. It is already embedded in mainstream AI tools that anyone can access.

What makes synthetic identity so dangerous is that it destroys the idea of trust at its foundation. In the past, fraud could be detected through inconsistencies. A forged signature might look wrong. A fake email might contain grammatical errors. A scam call might sound suspicious. Deepfake technology eliminates these clues. It creates perfect replicas that behave exactly like the person they are impersonating. When a deepfake CEO tells a finance manager to wire money, the face looks right, the voice sounds right, and the request fits the context. The attack does not feel like crime. It feels like business.

AI identity fraud has already caused massive financial and legal damage. Corporations have lost millions from deepfake video calls that instructed staff to transfer funds. Criminal rings have used voice cloning to impersonate family members and trick victims into sending emergency payments. Lawyers have received fake depositions. Journalists have been given fake interviews. Even biometric security systems have been bypassed by AI-generated fingerprints, faces, and voices. Every authentication method built on physical or behavioral traits is now vulnerable to synthetic replication. The speed of this threat is what makes it especially dangerous. AI models that once required advanced engineering skills are now available through simple web interfaces. A teenager with a laptop can clone a voice. A fraud ring can generate thousands of fake identities in minutes. State-sponsored actors can create propaganda videos that look completely real. The barrier to entry has collapsed, while the potential damage has exploded. This creates a perfect storm where identity itself becomes a weapon.

Social engineering has evolved into something far more sophisticated. Instead of guessing passwords or tricking people with fake emails, attackers now become the people they want to exploit. They speak in their voices, use their faces, and mimic their communication style. AI studies speech patterns, word choices, and emotional cues. It learns how someone expresses urgency, authority, or vulnerability. Then it reproduces those traits with precision. The victim is not just fooled. They are psychologically overridden by familiarity and trust.

In this new reality, digital forensics and cybersecurity must shift from verifying credentials to verifying authenticity. It is no longer enough to ask, "Is this the right password?" The question must become, "Is this really the person?" This requires analyzing micro-details that humans cannot see, such as unnatural blinking, audio phase distortion, or inconsistencies in muscle movement. AI must now defend against AI. The future of security will depend on machine-learning systems that can detect synthetic media faster than criminals can generate it.

Governments, financial institutions, and technology companies are racing to build authentication systems that cannot be easily copied. This includes cryptographic signatures embedded into video, blockchain-verified identity systems, and continuous biometric analysis that tracks liveness rather than static appearance. These defenses are still evolving, but they represent the next frontier in cybersecurity. The battle is no longer about protecting files and networks. It is about protecting reality itself.

Synthetic identity marks a turning point in human history. We are entering an era where digital representations are as powerful as physical presence. In the wrong hands, this technology becomes a tool for mass deception, financial theft, and political manipulation. In the right hands, it becomes a shield that restores trust in a world where nothing can be taken at face value. Understanding this shift is the first step toward surviving it.

"The Voice That Wasn't There"

The first time Elena realized something was wrong was when her father called her from a number she didn't recognize. His voice was exactly the same—warm, slightly hoarse, with the familiar pause before he spoke—but something about the urgency in his tone felt different. He told her he was in trouble, that he had been detained overseas and needed money sent immediately. He knew details only her father would know. He referenced memories, old jokes, even her childhood nickname. Elena felt her chest tighten as panic replaced logic.

She rushed to the bank, shaking as she prepared the transfer. The teller asked her a few questions, but Elena insisted it was an emergency. Her father had never asked for help like this before. She tried calling his regular phone, but it went to voicemail. The voice in her ear begged her not to hang up, to please hurry. Everything about it sounded real. Every emotional trigger was being pressed. She sent the money.

Three hours later, her father walked through her front door carrying groceries. He had never left the country. He had never made the call. The number was fake. The voice was AI. The money was gone.

Investigators later told Elena that her father's voice had been cloned from videos he had posted on social media. His speeches, family clips, and voice messages had been enough for an AI model to replicate him. The criminals had built a perfect digital ghost. They didn't steal his credit card. They stole his identity.

As the case expanded, authorities discovered that dozens of families had been targeted in the same way. Some had lost everything. Some had been blackmailed with fake recordings. Others had been tricked into revealing confidential data. The attacks were coordinated, automated, and powered by AI systems that ran continuously without human supervision. The criminals were not just running scams. They were running identity factories.

Elena joined a task force dedicated to stopping synthetic identity crime. She learned how deepfake detection systems analyzed voice frequencies, facial movements, and biological signals. She watched as AI models flagged subtle distortions invisible to the human eye. Every fake had a fingerprint. Every synthetic voice had hidden flaws. Technology that had created the threat was now being turned into the solution.

Months later, Elena received another call. It was her father's voice again, begging for help. But this time, she didn't panic. The detection software flagged the call instantly. The waveform didn't match a real human throat. The breath patterns were wrong. The deepfake was exposed before it could do any damage.

For the first time since the theft, Elena felt something return that she thought was gone forever: trust. In a world where anything could be faked, she had found a way to see what was real. And she knew that millions of others would need the same protection as the age of synthetic identity continued to spread.

The war against deepfakes had begun, not just in servers and algorithms, but in every human connection that depended on knowing who was truly on the other side of the screen.

Chapter 2

How Deepfakes Are Created

Deepfake technology begins with data. Every synthetic face, voice, or identity starts as a massive collection of real human material gathered from the internet, private devices, cloud accounts, and social media platforms. Photos, videos, voice notes, interviews, livestreams, voicemail recordings, and even video game voice chats are harvested to create training sets. The more material an attacker collects, the more accurate the resulting deepfake becomes. Modern AI does not need years of footage anymore. In many cases, just thirty seconds of clean audio or a few dozen high-resolution images are enough to generate a convincing digital clone.

Once the data is collected, it is fed into machine-learning models designed to extract patterns. For faces, the AI learns how the person's muscles move when they smile, blink, speak, or show emotion. It maps facial structure, eye movement, head tilt, and lighting response. For voices, the model analyzes pitch, tone, accent, breathing, rhythm, and emotional inflection. This process creates a mathematical blueprint of the individual. That blueprint can then be used to generate unlimited new content that looks and sounds exactly like the original person but is completely artificial.

Generative Adversarial Networks and transformer-based diffusion models are the engines behind most deepfakes. These systems use two competing neural networks: one that generates fake content and another that tries to detect whether it is real or fake. As they compete, the generator becomes increasingly skilled at producing content that fools the detector. Over thousands of iterations, the AI becomes capable of creating faces and voices that are indistinguishable from real ones. What once took days of processing now happens in seconds using cloud-based GPU infrastructure.

Real-time deepfakes have become one of the most dangerous evolutions of this technology. Instead of generating a video after the fact, AI can now modify a live video feed in real time. This allows attackers to appear on video calls as someone else, complete with facial expressions, lip movements, and eye contact. The victim sees what looks like a real person speaking directly to them. There is no delay, no obvious glitch, and no visible editing. It feels like a real human interaction because, from the user's perspective, it is.

Voice cloning operates in much the same way. A short audio sample is enough for AI to learn how a person speaks. The system can then generate new sentences in that voice, complete with emotional tone and natural pauses. This allows criminals to call banks, family members, and employees while sounding exactly like the person they are impersonating. In some cases, these voices have been used to defeat biometric voice authentication systems, granting attackers access to accounts and private data.

The final stage of deepfake creation is deployment. Criminals integrate their synthetic identities into automated attack systems. A single fraud ring can run thousands of fake phone calls, video conferences, and text conversations simultaneously. AI chatbots write the scripts. Voice generators deliver the speech. Video deepfakes provide the face. The operation becomes scalable, global, and relentless. There is no fatigue. No human hesitation. No moral restraint.

These attacks are often combined with traditional hacking. Stolen emails, leaked passwords, and breached databases give criminals context. The AI uses this information to craft believable conversations. It references recent transactions, real coworkers, and current events. The deepfake does not just look real. It behaves like someone who belongs inside the target's world. This is what makes it so effective.

The ability to fabricate identity on demand has transformed cybercrime into something far more powerful than hacking alone. It allows attackers to move freely through social systems that were built on trust. Deepfakes are not just technical tools.

They are social weapons. Understanding how they are created is the first step toward stopping them.

"The Face on the Screen"

When Marcus joined the investment firm, he never expected to face a threat that looked so familiar. One afternoon, he received a video call from the company's CEO. The man's face was perfect. His voice was calm but urgent. He explained that a confidential acquisition was underway and that funds needed to be transferred immediately. Marcus recognized every facial expression, every tone, every mannerism. There was no doubt in his mind that it was really him.

Marcus followed instructions and moved the money. Within minutes, it was gone. Hours later, the real CEO called asking why the funds had been transferred. Panic spread through the office as they realized what had happened. The call Marcus had seen was not a person. It was an AI-generated ghost.

Security experts were brought in. They analyzed the video and discovered microscopic inconsistencies in the way the eyes blinked and how the lighting reflected on the skin. The voice had a subtle synthetic resonance. To the human brain, it was invisible. To AI forensic tools, it was unmistakable. The company had been targeted because their executives frequently appeared in public videos and interviews. Their digital presence had been harvested and reconstructed. The attackers had built a flawless replica, then used it to bypass every internal control system.

Marcus struggled with guilt. He had trusted what he saw. He had trusted what he heard. But in this new world, those senses were no longer reliable. Only verification systems and digital fingerprints could separate truth from fiction.

Months later, when another fake call came in, the firm's new AI detection system caught it instantly. The deepfake was blocked before it could speak. Marcus watched as the software exposed the fraud in real time. A synthetic face, frozen and stripped of its power.

The war against identity theft had moved beyond passwords and firewalls. It was now a battle for reality itself—and Marcus knew he would never look at a screen the same way again.

Chapter 3

The New Age of AI-Powered Impersonation

The evolution of impersonation has reached a level that was unimaginable just a decade ago. In the past, criminals needed physical disguises, forged documents, or hacked email accounts to pretend to be someone else. Today, artificial intelligence allows them to become that person digitally. AI-powered impersonation is no longer about pretending—it is about replicating. When attackers use deepfake technology, they do not imitate a target; they reproduce them with extraordinary accuracy. This marks a fundamental shift in the nature of fraud, identity theft, and cybersecurity.

AI impersonation attacks operate at the intersection of psychology, technology, and social engineering. They exploit the way humans trust faces and voices. The brain is wired to believe what it sees and hears, especially when it comes from a familiar source. When an AI-generated version of a trusted person appears on a screen or speaks on the phone, the victim's defenses drop. Logic gives way to instinct. The attacker does not have to convince the target with arguments or threats; the identity itself becomes the weapon. Corporate environments have become one of the most profitable targets for AI impersonation. Executives are public figures within their organizations, appearing in training videos, webinars, and company meetings. Their faces and voices are easy to obtain. Once an attacker has enough material, they can generate fake video calls that appear to come from a CEO, CFO, or department head. These deepfake meetings are used to authorize wire transfers, reveal confidential data, or manipulate internal decisions. Employees who would never respond to a suspicious email will instantly comply with what looks like a direct order from their boss.

Financial institutions are also under siege. Voice authentication systems that were once considered secure are now being bypassed by AI-generated voices. Fraudsters call banks pretending to be customers, using cloned voices that match the bank's biometric records. These systems cannot distinguish between a real human and a synthetic replica. As a result, accounts are drained, credit lines are abused, and loans are issued to criminals using stolen identities that sound perfectly real.

Personal relationships have become another attack vector. AI impersonation is being used in romance scams, family emergency scams, and emotional extortion. A cloned voice can call a victim pretending to be a child, spouse, or parent in distress. The emotional impact is overwhelming. Victims act quickly, often sending money or sensitive information without verification. These crimes leave psychological scars far deeper than traditional financial fraud because the victim feels betrayed by someone they love—even though that person never actually spoke.

The political and social implications of AI impersonation are even more dangerous. Deepfake videos can show public officials making statements they never made. They can fabricate speeches, confessions, or threats. These videos can spread across social media in minutes, causing panic, market crashes, or violent unrest before they are debunked. The damage is often done long before the truth is established. In a world where any public figure can be digitally hijacked, stability itself becomes fragile.

The scale of AI impersonation is driven by automation. Criminals no longer need to target victims one at a time. AI systems can run thousands of fake conversations simultaneously. They can adapt in real time, responding to questions, changing tone, and escalating pressure. This creates a level of persuasion that no human scammer could achieve. The attacks are tireless, data-driven, and brutally efficient.

To combat this threat, identity verification must evolve beyond appearance and sound. Organizations are deploying multi-factor authentication, continuous biometric monitoring, cryptographic identity tokens, and AI-driven anomaly detection. Instead of asking, "Does this look right?" systems must ask, "Does this match the digital signature of a real human?" This includes analyzing micro-delays in speech, unnatural facial motion, and statistical anomalies in behavior. The future of trust will be mathematical, not visual.

AI-powered impersonation represents one of the greatest challenges to modern society. It threatens business, personal relationships, politics, and even the concept of truth itself. But it also forces a transformation in cybersecurity. By understanding how these attacks work, defenders can build systems that verify reality at a level deeper than the human senses. The battle ahead is not between people and machines. It is between deception and verification, between illusion and proof.

"The Man Who Wasn't Me"

Daniel first learned he had been cloned when his business partner called him in a panic. She had just spoken to Daniel on a video call, and he had ordered the release of sensitive financial documents. The problem was that Daniel had been in a meeting across town at the time. He had never made the call. Yet his face, his voice, and his mannerisms had all been there on her screen.

Security teams soon discovered that a deepfake version of Daniel had been operating for weeks. It had contacted employees, requested files, and slowly built a map of the company's internal systems. The AI had learned how Daniel spoke, how he smiled, and how he gave instructions. It knew his leadership style better than some of his own staff. To them, the fake Daniel felt completely real.

As the investigation continued, Daniel watched recordings of the deepfake impersonation. Seeing his own face speaking words he never said was deeply unsettling. The fake version of him was persuasive, confident, and precise. It had no fear, no hesitation, and no conscience. It was a perfect digital predator wearing his identity.

The company narrowly avoided a catastrophic data breach thanks to an AI detection system that flagged abnormal speech patterns. The deepfake was exposed seconds before it could execute a final command that would have transferred millions of dollars. The attack was stopped, but the damage to Daniel's sense of self was permanent.

From that day on, Daniel no longer trusted what he saw on screens. He adopted multi-layer identity verification for every interaction. Face, voice, and even behavior were no longer enough. Every communication now required cryptographic proof.

In a world where anyone could be digitally copied, Daniel realized that the only thing that truly defined him was not his appearance, but the invisible signatures that proved he was real. And those, finally, could not be faked.

Chapter 4

Detecting the Undetectable: How AI Finds Deepfakes

For years, the greatest advantage of deepfake technology was that it exploited the limits of human perception. Our eyes and ears are powerful, but they evolved to recognize faces and voices in the physical world, not in a digital environment where artificial intelligence can simulate reality with mathematical precision. Deepfake creators learned how to manipulate lighting, facial symmetry, voice tone, and movement in ways that tricked the human brain into believing something was real. But just as AI made deception more powerful, it also made detection more sophisticated. The battle against deepfakes is now being fought at the level of data patterns invisible to human senses.

Deepfake detection systems analyze digital media in ways humans never could. They do not rely on instinct or familiarity. They rely on physics, statistics, and biological truth. When a real person speaks, their voice contains micro-variations created by airflow, muscle tension, and the vibration of vocal cords. These produce subtle distortions that AI voices struggle to reproduce perfectly. Detection algorithms scan audio for unnatural frequency alignments, digital smoothing, and mathematical patterns that do not occur in human speech. Even the best AI voices leave behind hidden fingerprints.

Video deepfakes are exposed through similar techniques. Real human faces move in complex, imperfect ways. Tiny muscles contract and relax in patterns shaped by anatomy, emotion, and fatigue. AI-generated faces often miss these micro-movements or exaggerate them unnaturally. Detection systems analyze blinking rates, eye movement, jaw motion, and skin texture to identify inconsistencies. They also examine how light reflects off the skin and eyes. Synthetic images often produce lighting responses that are mathematically wrong, even if they look correct to the human eye.

Another powerful detection method is biological signal analysis. Real humans emit tiny color changes in their skin as blood flows beneath the surface. These changes are invisible to people but detectable to cameras and AI systems. This technique, known as remote photoplethysmography, allows software to detect heartbeats and breathing from video. Deepfakes cannot replicate these biological signals correctly, revealing their artificial nature. A fake face might look alive, but it does not pulse with real blood flow.

Behavioral analysis adds another layer of protection. Real people have natural timing when they speak, pause, and respond. AI systems, no matter how advanced, tend to operate with either unnatural consistency or algorithmic delays. Detection software measures reaction times, speech rhythm, and emotional pacing. When these patterns deviate from human norms, the system raises an alert. This allows security platforms to flag suspicious video calls, voice messages, and even text conversations.

Cryptographic verification is becoming one of the most important tools in deepfake defense. Some organizations embed digital signatures directly into legitimate video and audio recordings at the moment they are created. These signatures act like invisible watermarks that prove the content has not been altered. If a video or voice recording lacks a valid signature, it can be treated as untrusted. This approach shifts security away from guessing what is fake and toward proving what is real.

AI detection systems also use massive datasets of known deepfakes to train themselves. By analyzing millions of synthetic images, voices, and videos, detection models learn the unique artifacts that generative systems leave behind. Every AI model produces content in a slightly different way. These differences create a kind of fingerprint. As new deepfake tools emerge, detection systems are updated to recognize their signatures, creating an ongoing arms race between creators and defenders.

No single method is enough on its own. That is why modern deepfake defense uses layered verification. Audio analysis, video analysis, biological signals, cryptographic proof, and behavioral monitoring work together. When one system misses something, another catches it. This multi-layered approach is what makes it possible to protect banks, governments, corporations, and individuals from AI-powered identity fraud.

The future of deepfake detection will not rely on human judgment. It will rely on continuous, automated, AI-driven verification of reality. In a world where anything can be faked, trust must be built on data, not appearances. The war against synthetic identity will be won not by better eyes or sharper ears, but by smarter machines that know what real truly means.

"Seeing Through the Illusion"

Maya worked in cybersecurity for a global financial firm, but nothing prepared her for the day the CEO appeared on her screen and asked her to bypass a security protocol. His face was flawless. His voice carried authority and urgency. Yet something in the way he blinked felt wrong. It was too regular, too smooth, like a machine pretending to be human. Maya activated the company's deepfake detection system. As the CEO continued speaking, the software analyzed the video feed in real time. It measured light reflection on his skin, tracked eye movement, and searched for biological signals. Within seconds, red warnings began to flash. There was no detectable pulse beneath the synthetic face. The voice waveform showed digital smoothing. The man on the screen was not alive.

She ended the call and alerted security. The deepfake was traced to an overseas server farm running automated impersonation attacks. Hundreds of companies had been targeted, but Maya's firm was one of the few that had the technology to see through the illusion.

Later, the real CEO thanked her. He had never made the call. His identity had been stolen, but his company had been saved. Maya realized that in this new era, heroes were not just people with courage—they were people with the right algorithms.

As deepfakes continued to spread across the digital world, Maya and her team refined their systems, teaching machines to recognize truth at a level no human ever could. In a reality filled with perfect lies, they had built something more powerful: proof.

And for the first time, Maya felt confident that even in a world of illusions, reality could still be defended.

Chapter 5

Protecting Digital Identity in the Age of Deepfakes

Digital identity has become the foundation of modern life. It determines who can access bank accounts, healthcare records, corporate systems, and even government services. In a world where AI can perfectly replicate faces, voices, and behavior, protecting digital identity is no longer a matter of convenience—it is a matter of survival. Deepfake technology has turned identity into something that can be copied, altered, and weaponized. The challenge facing individuals and organizations is how to preserve authenticity in an environment where appearance is no longer proof.

The first layer of protection against AI identity fraud is moving beyond single-factor authentication. Passwords, PINs, and even biometric scans are no longer sufficient on their own. Voice authentication can be defeated by voice cloning. Facial recognition can be fooled by synthetic video. Instead, modern security systems rely on multi-factor and continuous authentication. This means verifying not just who someone is at login, but whether they remain the same person throughout an interaction. Behavioral patterns such as typing rhythm, mouse movement, speech cadence, and decision timing create a unique signature that is extremely difficult for AI to replicate perfectly.

Cryptographic identity is emerging as one of the most powerful defenses. In this model, every person, device, and piece of content is assigned a secure digital signature. When someone joins a video call, sends a message, or signs a document, their cryptographic key proves that the action came from a verified source. Even if a deepfake looks and sounds real, it cannot reproduce the underlying mathematical proof that confirms authenticity. This allows systems to automatically reject content that lacks valid verification.

Biometric liveness detection is another critical safeguard. Instead of simply scanning a face or voice, advanced systems look for signs of life. They measure blood flow, eye movement, breathing patterns, and muscle response in real time. A deepfake may produce a convincing image, but it cannot generate genuine biological signals. By continuously checking for these markers, security platforms can confirm that a real human is present and not an AI-generated replica.

Education is just as important as technology. People must be trained to verify identity even when something looks familiar. Organizations are now teaching employees to use verification codes, call-back procedures, and secondary confirmation channels before approving sensitive actions. Families are learning to use secret phrases or verification questions to protect against voice-cloning scams. Trust must be paired with proof, especially when money, data, or personal safety is at stake.

Regulatory frameworks are beginning to adapt as well. Governments are exploring laws that require AI-generated content to be labeled, watermarked, or cryptographically signed. Financial institutions are updating compliance standards to account for synthetic identity fraud. Courts are reconsidering what constitutes reliable evidence in a world where video and audio can be fabricated. These changes are slow, but they are necessary to maintain order in a digital society.

Organizations that survive the deepfake era will be those that treat identity as a living system rather than a static credential. They will use AI to monitor, analyze, and verify every interaction in real time. Instead of assuming trust, they will continuously measure it. This shift will define the next generation of cybersecurity.

Protecting digital identity is not about stopping technology. It is about using technology to defend what makes us human. In a world where anyone can be copied, authenticity becomes the most valuable asset of all. The future belongs to those who can prove who they are.

"The Key That Couldn't Be Copied"

Sophia nearly lost her company when a deepfake version of her appeared in a late-night video call. The fake Sophia calmly instructed her CFO to move funds into a "secure holding account." The face was perfect. The voice was identical. The mannerisms were unmistakable. But the transaction failed.

Her company had just implemented cryptographic identity verification. Every executive had a unique digital key that silently authenticated every communication. The deepfake had no key. The system flagged the call as unverified and blocked the transfer automatically.

Security teams traced the attack to an international fraud network that had successfully stolen millions from other firms. Sophia's company was one of the few that had upgraded its identity defenses in time.

When she watched the recording of the fake call, Sophia felt a chill. Seeing her own face speaking words she never said was like watching a ghost wear her skin. But she also felt a sense of power. The attackers had everything—her face, her voice, her reputation—but they did not have her digital identity.

From that day forward, Sophia became an advocate for identity security. She taught her employees and her family how to verify authenticity. She helped other companies adopt cryptographic proof and liveness detection. Slowly, the industry began to change.

In a world where AI could copy almost anything, Sophia knew one thing could not be faked: mathematical truth. And that truth was now the shield protecting her life and her business.

Chapter 6

The Human Element in AI Fraud Prevention

Technology is only part of the equation in defending against AI-powered identity fraud. While detection systems, biometric analysis, and cryptographic verification form the backbone of security, humans remain the most critical element. Even the most sophisticated deepfake detection software cannot anticipate every context in which identity might be exploited. Awareness, training, and proactive skepticism are essential for reducing risk in corporate, financial, and personal environments. Organizations that fail to integrate human judgment into their security framework leave themselves vulnerable, no matter how advanced their AI defenses may be.

Humans are unique in their ability to interpret nuance, context, and intent. A deepfake might perfectly reproduce a CEO's face and voice, but subtle inconsistencies in tone, phrasing, or behavior can alert an attentive employee. These are patterns that machines may struggle to detect in real time, particularly in live interactions. Staff trained to recognize warning signs—such as unusual urgency, requests outside standard procedures, or deviations from normal communication patterns—provide a first line of defense that complements automated systems. Human intuition, when combined with AI analysis, creates a synergy that is far more effective than either alone.

Training employees to handle AI identity fraud requires deliberate effort. It is not enough to provide generic warnings about phishing or cybersecurity. Organizations must simulate deepfake attacks, provide real-life examples, and educate staff on the latest techniques criminals are using. Scenario-based training, including role-play and interactive workshops, helps employees internalize red flags and develop instinctive responses. This preparation turns potential victims into defenders, capable of recognizing synthetic content even before automated systems can flag it.

The human element also extends to decision-making protocols. Multi-tiered approval processes, separation of duties, and dual-authentication for high-risk actions help prevent a single employee from being exploited by a deepfake impersonation. Even if an AI convincingly mimics a senior executive, no transaction or disclosure should proceed without additional confirmation channels. These controls are critical because humans, by nature, are susceptible to trust, authority bias, and emotional manipulation—exactly the vulnerabilities AI impersonators exploit. Awareness campaigns for individuals are equally important. Families, retirees, and social media users often become targets of AI-generated scams in the form of cloned voices, fake video calls, or synthetic social media profiles. Public education initiatives, guidance on authentication apps, and teaching verification habits—such as callback protocols, secret questions, and trusted secondary channels—help people defend themselves. In the same way that society learned to protect against email phishing and ransomware, individuals must now learn to protect against impersonation in the AI era.

Corporate culture plays a vital role in fostering vigilance. Employees should feel empowered to question suspicious requests, even if they appear to come from senior executives. Encouraging open communication, providing reporting channels, and rewarding caution reinforce the human layer of security. AI systems may flag anomalies, but humans interpret context, assign priority, and decide on action. Culture can amplify technical safeguards by embedding skepticism, verification, and procedural rigor into daily operations.

Finally, the human element ensures adaptability. AI attacks evolve rapidly, and static detection rules can quickly become obsolete. Human analysts study patterns of fraud, update verification protocols, and develop training for new tactics. In essence, humans are the strategic intelligence behind automated defenses. Without this oversight, even the most advanced technology may fall prey to creative and adaptive attackers. Protecting digital identity is not solely a technological problem—it is a human challenge, requiring judgment, education, vigilance, and a culture of trust verification.

"Echoes of Someone Else"

Elena had been a compliance officer for ten years, and she had faced her share of cyber threats. But nothing could have prepared her for the morning when the CFO called her, voice sharp and insistent. "Elena, I need you to approve the transfer immediately. It's an urgent acquisition. Don't ask questions, just act." She froze. The voice was hers—familiar, confident, and commanding. Yet something about the tone, the rhythm, the choice of words felt off. She had been impersonated. And she hadn't even realized it yet.

Her hands shook as she picked up the phone, debating whether to follow the instruction. But before she could act, her internal fraud-detection system beeped, warning her that the call was coming from an unverified channel. The system highlighted inconsistencies in speech cadence, small anomalies in pronunciation, and digital fingerprints that were impossible to forge. Elena realized she was staring at a voice clone: a synthetic version of her boss designed to trigger trust and urgency.

The AI deepfake had been running a coordinated attack for weeks, targeting senior employees across multiple departments. It had studied emails, recorded meetings, social media videos, and casual video messages to replicate the CFO's mannerisms and style. Every interaction had been calculated to condition staff into compliance. This was not just technology—it was a psychological weapon engineered for human vulnerabilities.

Elena activated the emergency verification protocol. She contacted the real CFO through a secondary channel, confirming that no transfer was scheduled. Her alert prevented the release of millions of dollars. The fake voice vanished, and the office settled into uneasy silence. Everyone had seen what could happen when human instinct was the first, and most crucial, defense.

Over the next days, Elena led a comprehensive training initiative. Employees practiced recognizing subtle anomalies in voices and video feeds, learning to verify authority through multiple channels. Role-playing exercises simulated deepfake scenarios where trust was weaponized, reinforcing the principle that verification must always come before action. Employees discovered that their intuition, when paired with AI monitoring, became a powerful filter against deception.

Despite the technology, the attackers adapted. They changed their tactics, producing synthetic interactions with even greater fidelity. But Elena and her team were ready. Continuous monitoring, cryptographic validation, and real-time behavioral analysis allowed them to identify attacks before harm could occur. Humans and machines worked together, each compensating for the weaknesses of the other.

Months later, a new deepfake attempt arrived. This time, a synthetic version of the CEO appeared on a conference video call, asking for sensitive project files. Employees paused. They followed procedure: verification codes, callback checks, and cross-references with real-time data. The attack failed. The AI had been fooled by human vigilance, just as much as by technological safeguards.

Elena reflected on the incident and realized a critical truth: in the age of AI impersonation, technology alone cannot protect identity. Humans provide judgment, intuition, and adaptability. They are the lens through which synthetic threats are filtered, the first line of recognition, and the last barrier to disaster. In a world where reality can be copied, altered, and weaponized, vigilance, education, and judgment remain the ultimate defense. Elena had learned that even the most convincing echo of someone else could never replace the presence of a vigilant mind.

Chapter 7

AI Fraud in the Corporate World: Case Studies and Lessons Learned

Corporate environments have emerged as prime targets for AI-powered identity fraud. The combination of hierarchical structures, high-value transactions, and complex communication networks creates fertile ground for attackers using deepfakes to impersonate executives, manipulate employees, and exfiltrate sensitive data. These attacks are no longer hypothetical; they are real, global, and increasingly sophisticated. Companies that ignore the threat of AI impersonation risk significant financial loss, reputational damage, and regulatory consequences.

Case studies reveal the patterns of these attacks. In one notable instance, a multinational firm lost several million dollars after an AI-generated video call instructed a regional manager to release funds to a fraudulent account. The deepfake replicated the CEO's voice and facial expressions with astonishing accuracy. Employees, conditioned by trust in authority, complied without question. Investigators later determined that the attackers had studied months of internal video meetings to perfect the clone, demonstrating that preparation and reconnaissance are critical elements of corporate AI fraud.

Another case involved a law firm that suffered a breach of sensitive client documents. AI-generated emails and video calls mimicked senior partners, requesting access to confidential files. Staff initially followed protocols but failed to verify the cryptographic signatures embedded in communications. The attackers leveraged social engineering tactics in combination with synthetic identity, showing that technology alone is not sufficient to prevent fraud. Multi-layered defenses, combining human verification, AI detection, and procedural safeguards, are necessary.

Financial institutions have also been targeted aggressively. Banks and investment firms increasingly rely on biometric voice authentication for high-value transactions. In one case, criminals cloned a client's voice using only a short sample of audio from public interviews and past phone calls. The AI-generated voice bypassed the bank's verification system and authorized significant fund transfers before the anomaly was detected. This incident highlighted the vulnerability of relying solely on single-factor biometric authentication and underscored the need for continuous monitoring and multi-factor approaches.

Insurance companies are experiencing similar challenges. AI-generated deepfakes have been used to fabricate claims, replicate the likeness of policyholders, and even simulate fraudulent witness testimony. By combining synthetic video, voice, and textual data, attackers can present a coherent, credible narrative that is difficult to dispute. Detecting these attacks requires an integrated approach that analyzes behavioral patterns, cross-references data with known records, and applies AI-powered anomaly detection.

Lessons from corporate cases point to several best practices. First, continuous education is essential. Employees must be trained to recognize deepfake threats, question unusual requests, and follow verification protocols. Second, layered verification processes should be implemented for high-risk transactions. Dual-authorization, callback verification, cryptographic checks, and AI-powered anomaly detection together create a robust defense. Third, monitoring of digital presence is vital. Companies must understand what public content exists about executives, employees, and systems, since attackers rely on this material to generate convincing impersonations.

Corporate governance plays a critical role in defending against AI identity fraud. Boards and executives must prioritize cybersecurity as a strategic risk, not merely a technical issue.

Policies must define procedures for handling deepfake attacks, assign accountability, and ensure rapid incident response. Legal and regulatory frameworks are evolving to address synthetic identity threats, and organizations that proactively implement detection and verification protocols will be better positioned to comply with emerging requirements.

Finally, collaboration between humans and AI is the key to resilience. While detection algorithms can identify subtle inconsistencies invisible to human eyes, humans provide judgment, contextual understanding, and adaptive thinking. AI can flag anomalies, but humans must interpret the findings, make decisions, and respond to incidents. By leveraging the strengths of both, organizations can mitigate the risks of deepfake fraud and protect their assets, reputation, and trust.

In sum, AI identity fraud is no longer science fiction. It is a present and growing threat in the corporate world. By studying real-world cases, implementing layered defenses, and fostering a culture of awareness and verification, companies can reduce their exposure and respond effectively to attacks. The lessons learned from these incidents underscore the urgent need for preparedness in an age where digital impersonation is not just possible—it is inevitable.

"The CEO Who Never Called"

It was early Monday morning when Anika, the chief operations officer of a multinational tech company, received a video call from the CEO. His face appeared on her screen, calm, confident, and familiar. He smiled warmly but with a sense of urgency that immediately raised her attention. "Anika," he said, "we have a sensitive acquisition. The transfer needs to be approved immediately. I trust you to handle this." Every instinct screamed urgency. Every fiber of her memory recognized the CEO's mannerisms, the slight tilt of his head, the cadence of his voice.

Anika paused. Something felt subtly wrong. Her internal sense of pattern recognition noted that the CEO had never spoken this way about urgency in prior communications. She accessed the company's anomaly detection dashboard on her screen. The system analyzed the video and voice feed, checking micro-expressions, blinking irregularities, and speech waveform inconsistencies. It highlighted several anomalies, though nothing was obvious to the naked eye. The red flags illuminated a chilling truth: the CEO was not really on the call.

The deepfake had been created with meticulous precision. Attackers had monitored months of recorded video calls, interviews, and public appearances of the CEO. AI had analyzed micro-expressions, speech tempo, hand gestures, and facial micro-movements to create a near-perfect replica. The fake CEO was designed to exploit human trust, authority bias, and procedural urgency. Anika realized she had just been targeted by one of the most sophisticated identity fraud operations she had ever encountered.

She activated the company's multi-layer verification protocol. Using a secondary secure channel, she confirmed the CEO's schedule. He had been in a boardroom hundreds of miles away, preparing for a meeting. The realization that her mind had been tricked into believing what she saw and heard was both terrifying and enlightening. Technology alone could deceive the senses, but human vigilance and verification protocols had prevented disaster.

Anika reported the incident to the cybersecurity team. They traced the source of the attack to a network overseas that had attempted hundreds of similar deepfake interactions against multiple companies. The attackers had been running automated AI systems, generating synthetic video and audio to mimic top executives. Their goal was clear: infiltrate corporate processes, bypass controls, and extract funds. Without anomaly detection and human oversight, millions of dollars could have vanished within minutes.

Over the following weeks, the company held extensive training sessions for all staff. Employees practiced deepfake recognition, verification workflows, and multi-factor authorization procedures. Scenario-based simulations included video calls, voice messages, and text-based impersonations. They learned to pause, verify, and cross-reference every unusual request. Human intuition, coupled with AI detection, became their most critical defense.

Despite these preparations, attackers evolved. The AI deepfakes became smoother, more convincing, and increasingly difficult to distinguish. But by continuously combining human judgment with AI analysis, anomalies were caught before they could cause damage. The team implemented cryptographic verification for all executive communications, behavioral analysis for all financial approvals, and continuous monitoring of digital presence to preempt impersonation attempts.

Months later, a similar attempt arrived. A synthetic video of the CEO appeared on the firm's conference call, requesting sensitive R&D documents. Staff immediately detected irregular micro-expressions, subtle speech pattern anomalies, and lack of cryptographic verification. The system flagged it instantly, and the communication was quarantined before any interaction occurred. The attackers had failed again.

Anika realized the lesson that would define her career: in a world of AI-generated deception, vigilance, protocol, and human judgment are irreplaceable. The CEO who never called had taught the company a critical truth: technology can mimic reality, but prepared humans can safeguard it. It was a war between replication and verification, between illusion and trust, and for the first time, she felt confident that her team could defend reality itself.

Chapter 8

The Future of AI Identity Fraud and Emerging Threats

As artificial intelligence continues to advance, the threat landscape for identity fraud is evolving at an unprecedented pace. Deepfake technology is becoming more accessible, more realistic, and more versatile, enabling attackers to fabricate not just faces and voices, but entire personas capable of interacting seamlessly with humans across multiple platforms. What was once considered experimental or futuristic has now become an operational reality, and organizations, governments, and individuals must prepare for a new era where trust is no longer guaranteed by appearance or sound.

Emerging threats extend beyond simple impersonation. AI can now synthesize body language, handwriting, and even emotional expression, creating digital representations that behave consistently across video, audio, and text channels. Imagine a synthetic executive participating in video conferences, sending emails, and conducting chat interactions—all appearing completely authentic. These AI-generated personas are designed to exploit social trust, circumventing traditional security measures that rely on visual or auditory recognition. The convergence of multi-modal deepfakes presents an entirely new class of risk for corporate, financial, and personal security.

The automation of these attacks is also a significant concern. Deepfake campaigns can now be executed at scale, targeting thousands of individuals or organizations simultaneously. AI-powered bots can interact in real-time, dynamically adjusting speech, tone, and behavior to manipulate responses. These automated attacks remove the limitations of human attackers, allowing fraudsters to maintain persistence, adaptability, and speed beyond traditional defenses. The sophistication of this technology means that victims often do not realize they are being deceived until it is too late.

Financial and regulatory implications of AI identity fraud are enormous. Banks, investment firms, and insurers increasingly rely on digital verification methods, many of which can be bypassed with high-quality synthetic content. Identity verification platforms, once considered secure, are vulnerable to the combination of multi-modal deepfakes and social engineering. Governments and regulators are beginning to recognize these threats, but legislation and compliance frameworks are struggling to keep pace with technological advancements. Organizations that fail to implement adaptive verification systems risk significant financial and legal exposure.

The psychological impact of synthetic identity attacks is equally profound. Victims often report feelings of violation, distrust, and anxiety, particularly when the attack involves intimate or personal interactions. Deepfakes blur the line between reality and illusion, making it difficult to distinguish between genuine and fabricated communications. This erosion of trust extends beyond individuals to entire organizations, where employees may second-guess the authenticity of colleagues, executives, or stakeholders. Maintaining confidence in human interactions becomes as important as safeguarding data and finances.

Countermeasures continue to evolve in response. Multi-factor verification, behavioral biometrics, cryptographic validation, and continuous AI monitoring form the foundation of modern defense strategies. Machine-learning models are trained not just to detect known deepfake patterns, but to anticipate new forms of synthetic behavior. Adaptive algorithms analyze inconsistencies in timing, frequency, and biological signals across all modalities. Organizations are also investing in employee training and awareness campaigns, teaching staff to question and verify unusual requests, even when they appear to come from trusted sources.

Looking to the future, the arms race between AI attackers and defenders will accelerate. Deepfake creation tools will become faster, more accurate, and easier to use, while detection and verification systems must become more sophisticated, intelligent, and responsive. The integration of quantum computing, advanced generative models, and real-time AI synthesis may enable even more convincing synthetic personas. Defending digital identity will require continuous innovation, collaboration across industries, and a holistic approach that combines technology, human judgment, and regulatory compliance.

Ultimately, the survival of trust in the digital age depends on our ability to adapt. AI identity fraud is not a passing threat; it is a structural change in how humans interact online and verify reality. Organizations that ignore this reality will face financial, reputational, and operational consequences. Those that embrace adaptive defenses, layered verification, and ongoing education will maintain resilience. The future of identity in an AI-driven world is uncertain, but with foresight, vigilance, and innovation, it is possible to protect what is real, even when deception looks perfect.

"The Phantom Executive"

Lucas had been the Chief Information Security Officer for over a decade, but nothing in his experience had prepared him for the attack that began on a quiet Tuesday morning. The company's Slack channels lit up with messages from the CEO, instructing employees to release confidential product designs to a new strategic partner. His tone was polite but insistent, his voice unmistakable. Every employee recognized it. Every interaction looked legitimate. Yet Lucas felt a deep unease. Something about the phrasing, the timing, and the frequency of the messages felt algorithmically precise, too perfect to be human.

He immediately initiated the company's verification protocols. Multi-factor authentication alerts and cryptographic identity checks were triggered. The AI detection system analyzed video and voice feeds simultaneously, searching for micro-expression inconsistencies, irregular blinking, and synthetic speech markers. Within seconds, the system flagged the communications as synthetic. The CEO had never sent the messages. They were the work of an AI-generated phantom, a digital replica designed to manipulate and deceive the organization.

The attackers had been patient. Over months, they had gathered audio recordings from public interviews, video of town halls, and casual conference call snippets. They fed these into a generative AI that created a multi-modal deepfake capable of sending texts, videos, and emails. The system learned behavioral patterns, adapting dynamically to employee responses, nudging them toward compliance. The phantom executive was relentless, persuasive, and terrifyingly real.

Lucas convened an emergency team. They traced the AI network, noting the scale and sophistication. Hundreds of employees had been targeted, each receiving personalized instructions designed to exploit their role, responsibilities, and previous interactions. The attackers had tested responses, optimized timing, and simulated urgency with uncanny precision. Every touchpoint was calculated, making detection by untrained staff almost impossible.

Training became critical. Employees participated in live simulations, recognizing subtle deviations in speech, timing, and body language. The team drilled protocols for cross-verifying requests, initiating callback checks, and analyzing cryptographic signatures. Lucas realized that while AI could replicate appearances, it could not mimic intuition, critical thinking, or procedural rigor. Human judgment, combined with technology, became the decisive defense.

Despite initial panic, the team managed to contain the attack. The phantom executive had been stopped before sensitive designs or financial assets were compromised. The event served as a wake-up call: the company's defenses had worked because humans and AI collaborated effectively, but the attackers had demonstrated a new paradigm of fraud, one that could adapt and evolve. Lessons learned had to be implemented immediately to prevent future breaches. Weeks later, Lucas reviewed a recording of the phantom's communications. The deepfake CEO moved and spoke perfectly, matching every known mannerism. Watching it was unnerving. Yet it also reinforced an essential truth: in a world dominated by synthetic replication, vigilance, verification, and human intuition were irreplaceable. Technology alone could not protect reality, but humans—trained, aware, and empowered—could see through even the most convincing illusion.

The phantom executive had been defeated, but Lucas knew the next attack would be more advanced, more difficult to detect. The arms race between AI fraud and identity protection was only beginning. He resolved to prepare, knowing that in a future where anyone could be copied, only those who combined human judgment with intelligent technology would survive—and thrive.

Chapter 9

Regulatory, Legal, and Investigative Approaches to AI Identity Fraud

As AI-powered identity fraud continues to escalate, governments and regulatory bodies are confronting the complex challenge of adapting existing laws to a world where digital identity can be perfectly fabricated. Deepfake technology undermines many traditional assumptions in legal proceedings, contract validation, and financial accountability. Courts and regulators are struggling to define evidence standards, liability frameworks, and compliance requirements in a landscape where visual, auditory, and behavioral cues can no longer be assumed authentic. Understanding the legal and investigative environment is critical for organizations and individuals seeking to protect themselves.

Current regulatory approaches vary widely by jurisdiction. Some countries have enacted laws explicitly criminalizing the malicious creation and distribution of deepfakes, particularly when used for fraud, defamation, or political manipulation. Others apply existing statutes, such as wire fraud, identity theft, cybercrime, and data protection laws, to prosecute attacks that involve AI-generated content. However, enforcement is often complicated by the cross-border nature of AI attacks. A deepfake created in one country can target victims in another, making jurisdictional authority, extradition, and evidence collection complex.

Financial regulators have also begun incorporating AI identity fraud into their compliance frameworks. Banks, investment firms, and insurance companies are required to implement systems that detect anomalies in transactions, communications, and authentication processes. Regulatory guidance increasingly emphasizes multi-factor verification, continuous monitoring, and employee training as essential safeguards. Firms that fail to implement adequate controls may face severe penalties, not only for financial loss but also for failing to protect customers against synthetic identity attacks.

Investigative methodologies are evolving alongside these regulatory initiatives. Digital forensics now includes techniques to analyze deepfake content, identify the generative AI model used, trace the origin of synthetic material, and uncover the network of operators behind attacks. Investigators examine micro-expression inconsistencies, voice waveforms, cryptographic signatures, and behavioral patterns across multi-modal data. These approaches allow law enforcement and corporate security teams to reconstruct attack pathways, attribute responsibility, and gather admissible evidence for prosecution. Privacy concerns also intersect with AI identity fraud regulation. Organizations must balance detection and verification practices with data protection and individual rights. Collecting and analyzing biometric, behavioral, or multi-modal identity data may raise legal questions about consent, storage, and sharing. Compliance frameworks such as GDPR in Europe, CCPA in California, and other emerging privacy laws require careful implementation of AI fraud detection systems to ensure legal and ethical use of personal data.

The legal implications extend to civil liability as well. Victims of AI identity fraud may pursue damages against individuals, corporations, or AI platform providers that facilitated or failed to prevent attacks. Cases have emerged where companies hosting AI creation tools have faced lawsuits alleging negligence in enabling malicious use. These legal pressures incentivize companies to adopt stricter controls, implement usage policies, and actively monitor for abuse of AI systems.

Finally, collaboration between private and public sectors is essential. Governments, financial institutions, technology providers, and cybersecurity firms must share intelligence on emerging attack methods, AI model vulnerabilities, and threat actor behavior. Regulatory bodies can mandate reporting standards, cross-border cooperation, and standardized investigation protocols, while companies implement practical safeguards. Together, these efforts create a layered defense against AI identity fraud, combining legal, technical, and investigative mechanisms to protect individuals, organizations, and society from increasingly sophisticated synthetic threats.

The legal and investigative landscape for AI identity fraud is still developing, but its trajectory is clear: AI impersonation is no longer a theoretical threat. It demands proactive legislation, enforceable compliance frameworks, advanced forensic capabilities, and cross-sector collaboration. Organizations and individuals who understand the intersection of technology, law, and investigation will be better equipped to navigate this complex, high-stakes environment and defend against the growing tide of synthetic identity crime.

"Courtroom of Shadows"

Detective Anya Morales had faced cybercrime cases before, but nothing as intricate or disorienting as the case that landed on her desk that March morning. A major political figure had been accused of authorizing controversial legislation based on a video recording that went viral online. The video showed the politician speaking with urgency, outlining directives in their own voice and using gestures familiar to millions of constituents. The problem: the politician insisted they had never made the statements, never even addressed the issue in question.

Anya began her investigation by analyzing the video frame by frame. Using AI forensic tools, she detected subtle inconsistencies in blinking patterns, lighting reflections, and skin micro-movements that indicated the video had been synthetically generated. The audio waveform contained unnatural harmonics and micro-pitch variations inconsistent with a human voice. It was a textbook deepfake. Yet the public impact had already been immense—social media posts, news articles, and commentary had spread the video to millions.

The investigation revealed the attackers had used generative adversarial networks trained on hundreds of hours of public footage, interviews, and speeches. These AI systems had learned not only the politician's facial features and voice but also their mannerisms, posture, and gestures. In essence, they had created a digital doppelgänger capable of acting convincingly across multiple mediums. The malicious actors had coordinated a sophisticated information campaign designed to manipulate public opinion and influence policy.

Anya coordinated with legal experts to navigate the complex jurisdictional challenges. The servers hosting the deepfake were located overseas, complicating evidence collection and potential prosecution. Using international legal assistance treaties, she obtained logs, metadata, and digital fingerprints that allowed attribution to a criminal group specializing in AI-driven disinformation. Forensics demonstrated the methodology, traced the generative model, and provided undeniable proof that the statements were fabricated.

Court proceedings were unprecedented. Judges and attorneys had to understand the technology behind the deepfake, its creation, deployment, and detection, in order to make informed rulings. Expert testimony described the AI model, the data it used, and the ways it could manipulate human perception. The defense highlighted how convincingly the deepfake mimicked reality, emphasizing the importance of clear standards of proof for synthetic content. Anya's team presented a comprehensive forensic report, showing that what appeared real to viewers was, in fact, entirely artificial.

The case set a landmark precedent for how courts handle AI-generated evidence. The judge ruled that digital content, regardless of apparent authenticity, must be corroborated through independent verification, cryptographic signatures, and forensic analysis. This established a legal standard for evaluating synthetic media in both criminal and civil proceedings, a crucial step toward regulating AI identity fraud.

The broader implications were profound. Political actors, corporations, and media companies began implementing new verification protocols, requiring cryptographic authentication for official communications and AI-assisted detection for sensitive media. Anya's work also led to international collaboration on standards for investigating AI impersonation, demonstrating that coordinated legal, technical, and investigative approaches were necessary to defend against synthetic identity attacks.

Months later, Anya reflected on the case. The courtroom had been filled with shadows—faces and voices that were not what they seemed. Yet through diligence, technology, and human judgment, truth had been restored. The deepfake had been exposed, the public informed, and a precedent set for future AI fraud cases. Anya understood that in a world where anyone could be digitally replicated, investigative rigor and legal innovation would be the pillars holding reality together. The shadows had been revealed, but the battle against AI identity fraud was only beginning.

Chapter 10

Preparing for the Future: Strategies to Mitigate AI Identity Fraud

The evolution of AI-powered identity fraud has fundamentally changed the landscape of cybersecurity. What once relied on simple phishing, password theft, or traditional impersonation has now advanced to a level where entire digital personas can be fabricated to deceive, manipulate, and extract value from individuals, organizations, and governments. Preparing for the future requires a holistic understanding of both technological and human factors, along with proactive strategies that anticipate the next generation of threats.

One of the most critical strategies is the integration of adaptive AI defense systems. These systems continuously learn from new attacks, analyzing patterns, inconsistencies, and subtle artifacts left by deepfake generation tools. By deploying machine-learning models capable of multi-modal analysis—examining video, audio, text, and behavioral data—organizations can detect synthetic content before it causes harm. This approach ensures that defenses evolve as attackers innovate, maintaining an edge in a constantly shifting threat landscape. Education and awareness remain fundamental pillars of preparation. Employees, executives, and even family members must understand the mechanics of deepfake technology, the methods attackers use to exploit trust, and the procedures for verification. Scenario-based training, regular workshops, and simulated attacks teach individuals to recognize anomalies, verify authenticity, and respond appropriately. Awareness empowers humans to act as the first line of defense, complementing automated detection systems.

Multi-factor and continuous authentication are essential. Traditional passwords or single biometric identifiers are no longer sufficient. Organizations must implement layered verification methods, combining cryptographic keys, behavioral biometrics, device authentication, and real-time anomaly detection. These layers create a defense-in-depth model, where even if one verification method is compromised, additional safeguards prevent unauthorized access. Continuous authentication further ensures that identity remains verified throughout the interaction, rather than only at the initial login or call.

Policy and governance also play a vital role. Clear procedures for handling high-risk transactions, reporting suspicious activity, and escalating potential fraud create organizational resilience. Compliance frameworks, both internal and regulatory, must address AI identity fraud, integrating standards for verification, record-keeping, and incident response. Governance also includes limiting access to sensitive information and monitoring digital footprints to reduce the availability of personal data that attackers might exploit.

Collaboration and information sharing are increasingly important. Cybersecurity is no longer a purely internal concern. Threat intelligence sharing between organizations, government agencies, and cybersecurity providers allows early detection of emerging attack patterns. By pooling knowledge, organizations can prepare for attacks before they are attempted, establishing best practices and standardized defense measures across industries.

Finally, future preparedness involves anticipating technological advancements. Quantum computing, next-generation generative models, and autonomous AI systems will make deepfakes faster, more realistic, and harder to detect. Organizations must invest in research, adopt forward-looking technologies, and maintain flexibility in their defense strategies. Success in this environment requires a combination of advanced AI detection, human vigilance, robust governance, and proactive adaptation to an evolving threat landscape.

Preparing for the future of AI identity fraud is a continuous process. The attackers will not pause; they will innovate, adapt, and seek new vulnerabilities. Organizations and individuals that combine technological sophistication, human insight, procedural rigor, and regulatory awareness will be best positioned to survive and thrive. In a world where appearances can no longer be trusted, the ability to verify reality itself will determine security, trust, and success.

"The Last Line of Verification"

It began with a seemingly innocuous email. Julian, the head of operations at a multinational energy company, received a request to approve an urgent fund transfer. The email appeared to come from the CEO, complete with signature blocks, corporate formatting, and a familiar tone. Julian's first instinct was trust—the message contained references to ongoing projects, recent meetings, and company-specific terminology. But something about the cadence of the language felt... off. Subtle differences, almost imperceptible, tugged at his intuition.

Julian activated the company's AI verification system. It analyzed the email's metadata, cryptographic signatures, and linguistic patterns. It cross-referenced the email against previously authenticated communications. Within seconds, the system flagged it as synthetic. The email was not from the

CEO—it was a highly sophisticated deepfake generated to manipulate trust and bypass procedural controls.

Realizing the gravity of the situation, Julian escalated the incident to the cybersecurity team. They traced the AI-generated communication to a coordinated criminal network operating from multiple countries, running automated attacks across dozens of companies. The attackers had compiled video, audio, and textual data from public interviews, meetings, and digital correspondence to perfect the CEO's digital persona. Their system was relentless, able to generate convincing interactions at scale, exploiting authority, familiarity, and urgency.

Over the next days, Julian led an emergency initiative to educate the entire company. Employees were trained to verify all communications through cryptographic checks, multi-factor confirmation, and secondary secure channels. Simulated deepfake attacks were conducted to reinforce procedures, highlighting how even experienced professionals could be deceived. The company culture shifted—trust became paired with verification, and intuition became a strategic tool in conjunction with technology.

As attacks persisted, the AI detection systems evolved as well. Continuous machine-learning models analyzed video, audio, and text for subtle anomalies: unnatural micro-expressions, digital frequency irregularities, inconsistencies in speech rhythm, and behavioral deviations. The synergy between human vigilance and AI intelligence became a critical defense. Each employee became a node in a verification network, ensuring that no single point of failure could allow unauthorized action.

One morning, a video call appeared on Julian's secure platform. It showed the CEO, speaking calmly, asking for access to confidential design files. The visuals and audio were flawless. The system immediately flagged irregular micro-expressions and missing biometric signatures. Julian paused, verified the cryptographic proof, and confirmed the request through a secondary channel. The deepfake was blocked. Employees watched in awe—what could have seemed like an authentic interaction had been neutralized before damage occurred.

Months later, Julian reviewed the lessons learned. Attackers would continue to innovate, and deepfakes would grow more sophisticated. Yet the company was prepared. Human judgment, adaptive AI detection, layered authentication, and procedural rigor had combined to form a robust defense. In this new world, where reality could be replicated perfectly by machines, the last line of verification—the combination of human insight and technological verification—had saved the organization from potentially catastrophic consequences. Julian understood that vigilance, training, and proactive adaptation were no longer optional; they were the foundation of security in the age of AI identity fraud.

Final Thoughts

As we reach the conclusion of this comprehensive guide to deepfake detection and AI-powered identity fraud, it is clear that the challenges of the digital age extend far beyond technical sophistication. Deepfake technology is no longer a niche concern for cybersecurity professionals—it is a pervasive threat impacting individuals, corporations, governments, and societies worldwide. The capacity to replicate human identity digitally has changed the very nature of trust, making verification and vigilance more critical than ever.

Throughout this book, we have examined how deepfakes are created, deployed, and weaponized. We have explored the technical underpinnings of AI-generated images, videos, and voice cloning, as well as the psychological and social engineering tactics used to exploit human trust. We have analyzed real-world corporate incidents, legal precedents, and investigative strategies that illustrate the breadth and impact of synthetic identity fraud. Each chapter has provided actionable insights, combining technology, human judgment, and procedural safeguards to equip readers with the tools necessary to defend against these threats. One of the most important takeaways is the interplay between humans and technology. AI is both a threat and a solution. Deepfake creators exploit human instincts and biases, but detection, verification, and authentication systems also rely on AI to analyze patterns invisible to the human eye. The combination of adaptive machine learning, behavioral analysis, and human intuition creates a defense structure capable of mitigating even the most sophisticated attacks. Understanding this synergy is fundamental to surviving and thriving in an AI-driven digital landscape.

Regulatory, legal, and investigative measures are essential complements to technical defenses. As deepfakes become more widespread, governments are developing laws to criminalize malicious AI content, financial regulators are establishing compliance frameworks, and law enforcement agencies are expanding forensic techniques to attribute responsibility and preserve evidence. Organizations that proactively integrate these regulatory insights into their cybersecurity strategies gain a crucial advantage, reducing exposure and enhancing trust with clients, partners, and stakeholders.

Education and culture are equally critical. Human awareness, procedural rigor, and an organizational culture that values verification over blind trust are indispensable tools in defending against synthetic identity attacks. Employees must be trained to recognize anomalies, challenge unusual requests, and apply multi-factor authentication consistently. Individuals should adopt verification habits for personal communications, understanding that AI can now replicate voices, faces, and even emotional cues with alarming accuracy. The human element remains the ultimate safeguard in a world where appearances can be faked.

Looking to the future, the arms race between attackers and defenders will accelerate. Advances in generative AI, real-time deepfakes, multi-modal impersonation, and autonomous AI systems will continue to challenge our ability to discern reality from fabrication. Organizations and individuals must remain proactive, continuously updating technology, policies, and education programs. Adaptability, vigilance, and a commitment to layered defense will define the leaders in cybersecurity for decades to come.

Ultimately, the core message of this book is clear: identity is the most valuable asset in the digital age, and defending it requires a multi-layered approach combining AI, human judgment, procedural rigor, and regulatory awareness. The threats are real, sophisticated, and evolving—but so too are the tools, strategies, and insights to counter them. By understanding the mechanics of deepfakes, implementing layered defenses, and cultivating vigilance, we can protect what is authentic, safeguard trust, and navigate the future of

AI with confidence. The battle may be complex, but the solutions are within reach for those willing to prepare, adapt, and act.

www.ingramcontent.com/pod-product-compliance
Ingram Content Group UK Ltd.
Pitfield, Milton Keynes, MK11 3LW, UK
UKHW021240300926
15471UKWH00014B/900

9 798295 598418